W9-AQZ-633

ESP

by Jacqueline Laks Gorman

Gareth Stevens Publishing
A WORLD ALMANAC EDUCATION GROUP COMPANY

J133.8
GOR

Please visit our web site at: www.garethstevens.com
For a free color catalog describing Gareth Stevens Publishing's
list of high-quality books and multimedia programs,
call 1-800-542-2595 (USA) or 1-800-387-3178 (Canada).
Gareth Stevens Publishing's fax: (414) 332-3567.

Library of Congress Cataloging-in-Publication Data

Gorman, Jacqueline Laks, 1955-
    ESP / by Jacqueline Laks Gorman.
        p. cm. — (X science: an imagination library series)
    Includes bibliographical references and index.
    Summary: Introduces different types of extrasensory perception, with examples
of precognition, psychokinesis, and clairvoyance.
    ISBN 0-8368-3198-5 (lib. bdg.)
    1. Extrasensory perception—Juvenile literature. [1. Extrasensory perception.]
I. Title. II. Series.
BF1321.G67   2002
133.8—dc21
                                   2002022521

First published in 2002 by
Gareth Stevens Publishing
A World Almanac Education Group Company
330 West Olive Street, Suite 100
Milwaukee, WI 53212 USA

Text: Jacqueline Laks Gorman
Cover design and page layout: Tammy Gruenewald
Series editor: Betsy Rasmussen
Picture Researcher: Diane Laska-Swanke

Photo credits: Cover © Dr. Susan Blackmore/Fortean Picture Library; pp. 5, 13 (main) NASA;
p. 7 © Bettmann/CORBIS; pp. 9, 13 (inset), 17 © Mary Evans Picture Library; pp. 11, 19
© Guy Lyon Playfair/Fortean Picture Library; p. 15 © North Wind Picture Archives; p. 21
© Fortean Picture Library

This edition © 2002 by Gareth Stevens, Inc. All rights reserved to Gareth Stevens, Inc. No part of
this book may be reproduced, stored in a retrieval system, or transmitted in any form or by any means,
electronic, mechanical, photocopying, recording, or otherwise without the prior written permission of
the publisher except for the inclusion of brief quotations in an acknowledged review.

Printed in the United States of America

1 2 3 4 5 6 7 8 9 06 05 04 03 02

Front cover: In a ganzfeld **experiment**, a person alone in one room tries to send thought messages to someone in another room.

TABLE OF CONTENTS

Words that appear in the glossary are printed in **boldface**
type the first time they occur in the text.

STRANGE HAPPENINGS

Did you ever have a dream that something would happen — and then it did? Did you ever know who would be on the other end of the phone line before you answered it? Did you ever know what someone was going to say before they said it? If so, you may have ESP.

ESP stands for extrasensory perception. That means getting information about people, places, events, and things without using the five senses of seeing, hearing, smelling, tasting, and touching. Sometimes ESP is called the "sixth sense."

Astronaut Edgar Mitchell did ESP **experiments** during the Apollo 14 mission to the Moon in 1971. He tried to send his thoughts back to Earth.

DIFFERENT TYPES OF ESP

There are four different types of ESP — telepathy, clairvoyance, precognition, and psychokinesis. Telepathy is mind reading or knowing someone else's thoughts. Clairvoyance is knowing about something by getting a sudden feeling about it or dreaming about it. Precognition is the ability to see the future. Psychokinesis is sometimes called "mind over matter" and means being able to move or change objects with your thoughts.

All of us may be born with some ESP, but we might not know it. The people who do best in ESP experiments believe in ESP and are interested in it.

Psychic Jean Dixon said she could predict the future. She said she knew years before he became president that John Kennedy would be killed. She tried to warn him in November 1963, the month he died.

THE FATHER OF ESP

Dr. Joseph Banks Rhine became the "father of ESP" in the 1930s. Rhine and his wife did many scientific studies of ESP in their laboratory at Duke University in North Carolina.

Many of these studies included experiments that used special cards called Zener cards. These cards have special symbols on them. Sometimes a person, called a **subject**, would try to guess the order of the cards in a shuffled deck. Other times, one person would look at a card and try to send a thought message about it to another person.

Some of Dr. Rhine's subjects did very well. Rhine said the subjects that did well could not have guessed the right answers so many times and that those subjects had ESP.

In one of Dr. Rhine's experiments, a subject tried to use her **mental** powers to make dice fall a certain way. In other experiments, subjects tried to predict how dice would fall from a special machine that tumbled them out.

ESP RESEARCH

Dream research is another way scientists study ESP. The subject goes to sleep, while a second person in another room watches films. The person watching films tries to send thought messages about the films to the sleeping subject. The subject wakes up and describes what he or she dreamed. If the subject had ESP, he or she would have dreamed about the films.

Another kind of ESP research is called a "ganzfeld experiment." Here, the subject relaxes in a quiet room. A person in a different room looks at pictures and tries to send thought messages about the pictures to the subject. Later, the subject describes what he or she saw and whether the actual pictures look like the messages he or she received.

A subject gets ready to take a ganzfeld experiment. There can be no **distractions**. The subject's eyes are covered, and she wears headphones that play relaxing sounds.

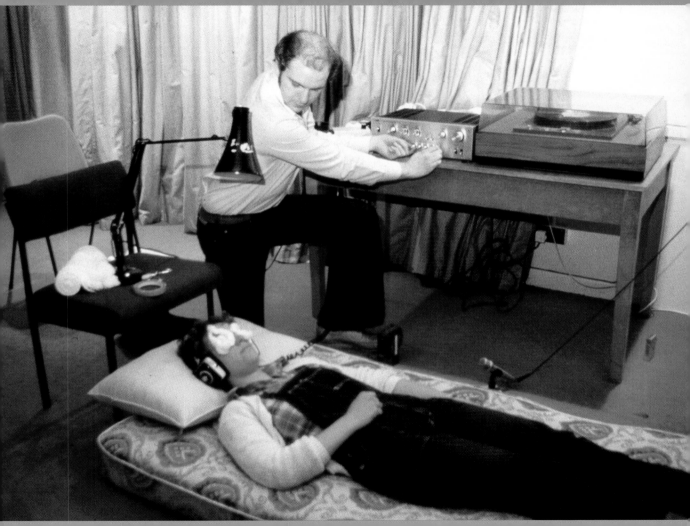

THE CASE OF INGO SWANN

Ingo Swann is an artist who can do amazing psychic things, one of which is **remote viewing**. Swann can describe things that are far away. He does this by going into a **trance**. Swann says his mind floats away, looks at distant objects, and then returns to his body.

In 1973, Swann worked with scientists to do a remote viewing of the planet Jupiter. Swann described Jupiter and made drawings of what he saw. Months later, the spacecraft *Pioneer 10* sent information about Jupiter back to Earth. Years after that, the spacecraft *Voyager 1* sent back more information. Many of Swann's descriptions about Jupiter were correct.

Ingo Swann has had ESP experiences since he was a child. In 1973, he described the planet Jupiter for scientists. He correctly said that Jupiter has a ring around it, has **hydrogen** in its **atmosphere**, and has mountains and strong winds.

KNOWING THE FUTURE THROUGH DREAMS

In 1979, a man named David Booth began having terrible dreams about a plane crash. Booth had the nightmare every night for ten nights and warned the government. He had his last dream on May 24 of that year. The next day, May 25, a jet crashed in Chicago, killing 275 people. The accident happened just as it had in Booth's dream.

Other people have **predicted** the future with dreams. In the 1850s, writer Mark Twain dreamed about his brother's coffin. He even saw the types of flowers on it. A few weeks later, Twain's brother died in an accident. All of the details Twain had seen in his dream came true.

President Abraham Lincoln told some people about a dream he had, about people crying in the White House. They were around a coffin and told him the president had been murdered. A few weeks later, Lincoln was shot and killed.

© North Wind Picture Archives

PSYCHIC DETECTIVES

Some psychics work with the police on difficult cases. These psychics help find missing people or people who have been kidnapped. The psychics may get feelings about where the missing people are by looking at pictures of them or holding their clothing. Sometimes the psychics help police figure out who murdered someone.

The United States government has also used psychics in different ways. Some psychics have helped the government find American prisoners. Some psychics say they even worked as spies for the government to collect useful information, such as the location of enemy submarines, military targets, or weapons.

Gerald Croiset was a well-known clairvoyant who often helped the Dutch police. He helped solve crimes and find missing people. His son also has psychic powers.

IS ESP REAL?

Does ESP really exist? Some people say it does not. These people say that ESP can be explained by coincidences, misunderstandings, wishful thinking, or imagination. They also say that some psychics are fakes who are just pretending to have powers.

People who believe in ESP, however, say that we just don't know everything about the world. Our minds, the things around us, and space and time may be connected in some very important ways that we do not yet understand.

Uri Geller is a psychic from **Israel** who claims that he can do many things with his mind, like bend metal objects and stop watches from working. Many scientists say that he is a fake who is only doing tricks.

DO YOU HAVE ESP?

To find out if you have ESP, keep an ESP journal. When the phone rings, write down the name of the person you think is calling. Answer the phone, and then write down the caller's name. After a few weeks, see how often you were right. You can also write down your dreams when you wake up and later see if they came true.

You could also experiment with Zener cards with your friends. Shuffle the cards well. Pick up a card and concentrate on the symbol. Try to send a thought message about it to your friend. Your friend should write down what he or she thinks the card is. Do this 100 times. If your friend is right more than 60 times, he or she might have ESP.

Zener cards are printed with five symbols — a star, a circle, a cross, wavy lines, and a square. The cards were created by Dr. Karl E. Zener, who did early ESP experiments while working with Dr. Rhine.

MORE TO READ AND VIEW

Books (Nonfiction)

ESP: Are You a Mind-Reader? Elements of the Extraordinary (series). Andrew Boot (Harper Collins)

ESP. Mysteries of Science (series). Elaine Landau (Millbrook Press)

Scary Science: The Truth Behind Vampires, Witches, UFOs, Ghosts and More! Sylvia Funston (Owl Books)

What's So Super About the Supernatural? Robert Gardner (Twenty-First Century Books)

Books (Fiction)

Danger at the Fair. Peg Kehret (Pocket Books)

Elvis the Turnip . . . and Me. The Zack Files (series). Dan Greenburg (Grosset & Dunlap)

ESP TV. Mary Rodgers (HarperCollins)

I'll See You in My Dreams. Ilene Cooper (Viking)

I'm Out of My Body . . . Please Leave a Message. The Zack Files (series). Dan Greenburg (Grosset & Dunlap)

This Body's Not Big Enough for Both of Us. The Zack Files (series). Dan Greenburg (Grosset & Dunlap)

Yikes! Grandma's a Teenager. The Zack Files (series). Dan Greenburg (Grosset & Dunlap)

Videos (Nonfiction)

History's Mysteries: America's Psychic Past. (History Channel)

Secrets of the Unknown: Dreams and Nightmares. (MPI Home Video)

Secrets of the Unknown: Psychic Detectives. (MPI Home Video)

The Unexplained: Modern Psychics. (A&E)

WEB SITES

Web sites change frequently, but we believe the following web sites are going to last. You can also use good search engines, such as **Yahooligans!** [www.yahooligans.com] or **Google** [www.google.com] to find more information about ESP. Some keywords that will help you are: *ESP, telepathy, clairvoyance, precognition, psychokinesis,* and *Zener cards*.

www.ajkids.com

Ask Jeeves Kids, the junior Ask Jeeves site, is a great place to do research. Try asking:

What is extrasensory perception?

What is telepathy?

You can also just type in words and phrases with "?" at the end, such as:

Paranormal?

www.yahooligans.com

This junior version of the Yahoo site is very easy to use. Simply type in the letters "ESP" to get a list of sites that are appropriate for kids.

www.aspr.com

This site of the *American Society for Psychical Research* supports the scientific investigation of ESP.

www.psiresearch.org

This is the site of the *Consciousness Research Laboratory*, which conducts scientific research on ESP. Questions about psychic topics are answered, and you can even take some online tests to discover your own psychic ability.

www.randi.org

The *James Randi Education Foundation* was set up by James Randi, a famous magician. He is the world's leading investigator of what he calls "pseudoscience." He tries to prove that most paranormal and supernatural things are not real.

www.rhine.org

This is the site for the *Rhine Research Center & Institute for Parapsychology*, which continues the pioneering work of Dr. Joseph Banks Rhine.

www.paranormal.about.com

This *Paranormal Phenomena* site has reports on different ESP topics, or you can explore such things as automatic writing, channeling, Ouija board, out-of-body experiences, paranormal people, and remote viewing.

GLOSSARY

You can find these words on the pages listed. Reading a word in a sentence helps you understand it even better.

atmosphere (AT-mah-sfeer) — the air around a planet. 12

distractions (dihs-TRAK-shuns) — things or thoughts that draw attention away from what you are trying to concentrate on. 10

experiments (eks-PEER-ih-mehnts) — tests performed in order to learn more about an idea. 4, 6,8, 10, 20

hydrogen (HY-droh-jihn) — a colorless, odorless gas. 12

Israel (IHS-ray-ehl) — a small country near the Mediterranean Sea. 18

mental (MEHN-tuhl) — of the mind. 8

predicted (pree-DIK-tehd) — to have known what will happen before it happens. 14

psychic (SY-kik) — relating to the human mind, or someone with ESP ability. 6, 12, 16, 18

remote viewing (ree-MOHT VYOO-een) — the ability to see faraway objects by having the mind leave the body. 12

subject (SUHB-jekt) — a person being studied or examined. 8, 10

trance (TRANSS) — a sleeplike state. 12

INDEX